FIELD MANAGEMENT

by
Mary Gordon Watson

Illustrations by
Carole Vincer

KENILWORTH PRESS

First published in Great Britain by
Kenilworth Press Limited,
Addington, Buckingham, MK18 2JR

© Kenilworth Press Limited 1994

First edition, under the title *Fields and Fencing*, published in 1988
This second edition, under the new title *Field Management*, published in 1994
Reprinted 1996 and 2002

British Library Cataloguing in Publication Data
A catalogue record for this book is available from the British Library.

ISBN 1-872082-49-1

Typeset by Kenilworth Press Limited

Printed in Great Britain by Westway Offset

CONTENTS ■ ■ ■ ■ ■ ■ ■ ■ ■ ■ ■ ■ ■ ■

Introduction

It is more natural to keep a horse or pony in a field than to confine him in a stable, but not every horse will thrive living out at grass all the time, as conditions are seldom ideal and they are very different from his original habitat.

In the wild, he could wander freely to look for essential water and food, and to find shelter in very wet, cold and windy weather, or in strong sunshine. The natural grease in his ungroomed coat gave further protection against the elements, and also against flies. His travel kept his feet trimmed.

A horse will seldom choose to be alone: he feels happier and more secure in a herd or paired with a companion.

However, without our help and regular attention, a horse or pony enclosed in a field would be deprived of many of these basic necessities.

This book offers practical advice on basic pasture management, with tips on maintenance which will help to keep your fields in good condition and free from hazards and weeds. It shows that if you take good care of your field and the fences that surround it, you can avoid unnecessary accidents, disease, or other distress, and your horse is more likely to remain both happy and healthy.

Fields – the four seasons

A field, or paddock, or pasture, is an enclosed area of grassland where horses or ponies may spend up to 24 hours a day. It may be the only place available to them for food and exercise.

Many horses are limited to one small field, which if grazed all of the time will soon become horse-sick and useless. It is much better to divide the area into three parts so that it can be grazed/treated/rested in rotation.

A minimum size of one acre per horse is a general rule, but this largely depends on the quality of the grazing and its management: weed and worm control, good drainage, applying fertiliser or other necessary treatment, periodic resting.

Field conditions vary greatly according to the weather and seasons.

In winter, grass has no food value, and it may be frozen or under snow. Even the toughest ponies or horses, whether being worked or not, will need extra food to keep warm and healthy.

In spring, the grass starts growing, and it is at its best from May to July. Horses must not eat too much too quickly.

Summer is a suitable time to rid a field of harmful or useless vegetation, to top or cut coarse, unwanted areas, and to harrow the land.

In autumn, the grass may grow a little, but if horses are standing about looking hungry they may need hay - and they will soon let you know how much to feed them.

A suitable field

The physical and mental well-being of any horse or pony depends very much on his surroundings. If he lives out in a field, his basic needs will be:
- A plentiful supply of fresh water.
- Nourishing grass, with extra food when necessary.
- Companionship - preferably with other horses.
- Shade and shelter.

A contented horse is unlikely to want to jump out of his field or chew the fences or trees or nibble at harmful vegetation because he is bored or hungry. He is also less likely to quarrel with his companions.

Most horses will benefit from a periodic change of field. New surroundings can prevent the formation of bad habits such as crib-biting, or walking up and down the fence line.

Meanwhile, the 'used' field can be rested, treated if necessary, or grazed down by cattle.

Horses in a field should be looked over every day, and the fences should be checked. Any weak places, such as loose nails or wire, should be dealt with before they become a potential danger. Droppings should be removed regularly, and weeds pulled up and burned.

The quality of grassland can deteriorate rapidly, especially when over-grazed, and if it becomes horse-sick it will take months or even years of treatment and rest to restore its usefulness. Horses do not thrive on sour, foul-tasting pasture, or in muddy, bog-like conditions.

Good field management may take up more time and money but you will save on extra food, veterinary bills, and the effort it takes to get your horse fit.

An unsuitable field

A neglected horse in a neglected field is an ugly sight. It gives the horse owner a bad name - and he deserves it!

A captive horse is completely dependent on what he finds in his field. Water is vital to all his bodily functions. Dirty, contaminated water is not acceptable. It must be checked for dead insects, birds or other animals, leaves, or any unwanted matter. In very wet, cold weather, the horse needs shelter, and when it is very hot and the flies are troublesome he will need shade. A thick, bushy hedge is much better than an unsuitable shed.

A sick field will have bare, grazed patches and rough areas of inedible grass or weeds which horses will not touch. Harmful weeds and plants are a sure sign of bad management and unhealthy horses, and worm infestation from droppings is a severe problem.

Horses dislike being alone, but overstocking will soon ruin a field. Also, when they are hungry or bored they tend to fight.

Field hazards which could lead to injury include:
♦ Dangerous, weak, or inadequate fencing and gates.
♦ Sharp objects such as nails, metal posts, barbed wire or wire ends, discarded machinery.
♦ Unprotected cables or pylons.
♦ Litter, such as bottles and cans thrown into the field.
♦ Rabbit holes, bogs, 'blind' ditches, or treacherous ground which may be too stony, slippery, or steep.

Types of fencing

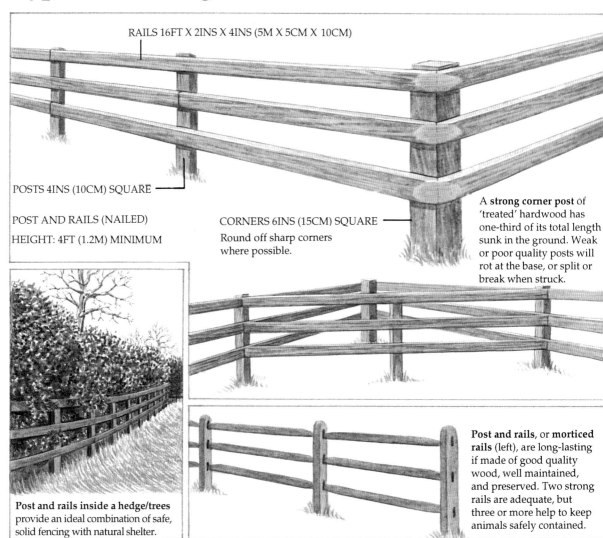

RAILS 16FT X 2INS X 4INS (5M X 5CM X 10CM)

POSTS 4INS (10CM) SQUARE

POST AND RAILS (NAILED)
HEIGHT: 4FT (1.2M) MINIMUM

CORNERS 6INS (15CM) SQUARE
Round off sharp corners
where possible.

A **strong corner post** of
'treated' hardwood has
one-third of its total length
sunk in the ground. Weak
or poor quality posts will
rot at the base, or split or
break when struck.

Post and rails inside a hedge/trees
provide an ideal combination of safe,
solid fencing with natural shelter.

Post and rails, or **morticed
rails** (left), are long-lasting
if made of good quality
wood, well maintained,
and preserved. Two strong
rails are adequate, but
three or more help to keep
animals safely contained.

The fencing around a field or paddock
must be safe, strong and high enough
to contain horses. If it is lower than 4ft
(1.2m), a horse might be tempted to jump
out, or he may lean on it with his chest,
which would weaken or break it. In
spring and autumn when their coats are
changing, horses will rub hard against
anything convenient such as posts or
gates. Posts will last much longer if made
of good quality timber and tanalised or
impregnated with preservative.

A natural hedge provides shade and
shelter, but to be stockproof, it should
be thick, at least 5ft (1.5m) high and 3ft
(about 1m) wide, with no weak places. It
will need trimming and must not contain
poisonous plants such as yew, laurel or
laburnum.

A natural bank and ditch may not be
enough to keep horses in their field, but
dry stone walls make excellent fencing

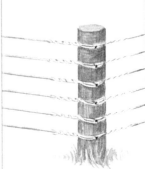

Rail and diamond mesh wire is very safe and strong. It is expensive, stock-proof and requires minimal maintenance.

Plain wire provides effective fencing if it is well erected and kept tensioned. Strands should be about 1ft (0.3m) apart, while a top rail increases safety and strength. A **corner post** needs **strainers**, or **'droppers'**, to keep it firm and upright, and to support the fences on either side. A weak corner makes the fencing insecure and unsafe.

Polyamid fencing does not conduct electricity. It is easy to handle and to transport, stays smooth and does not sag or corrode.

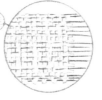

A **gatebreak** attaches an 'active' wire or tape to a buckle, to make an opening or gate. The insulated handle has an external spring which tensions the wire or tape.

Polyethylene tape, available in white, brown or green, is light and easy to handle. The widest variety (40mm), contains 15 filaments of .33mm stainless-steel wire, interwoven with thick nylon. A small energiser activates it.

Insulators

An **'active' tape fence** is flexible, strong, visible and versatile. Wide tape needs support from light stakes every 16ft (5m), with stronger posts and a tensioner at corners or gateways. Two strands are sufficient. It must be well insulated and the posts heeled in. Avoid sharp angles in corners .

A **portable battery energiser** has its own stand as an earth rod. It is easily moved from field to field.

A **high-power battery energiser** is suitable for large fields. A 12-volt battery must be very well earthed and the current tested.

if high enough and well maintained.

Plain wire with a top rail provides good practical, and fairly economical fencing. It is safer than a plain wire fence which tends to stretch. Also, it can be difficult to see, and could cause cuts and injuries, particularly when loose. Wooden posts are preferable to unyielding metal or concrete. Where a temporary fence is useful, an electric fence of wire or tape is often practical: it is portable, efficient and cost effective.

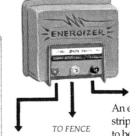

TO BATTERY

TO FENCE

TO EARTH

An electric fence, often a single strip of Polywire, enables a field to be strip grazed or an area to be rested . It separates horses in adjoining fields, and can be used with other fencing to keep horses off weak/dangerous areas or to prevent chewing or jumping out.

Types of fencing cont.

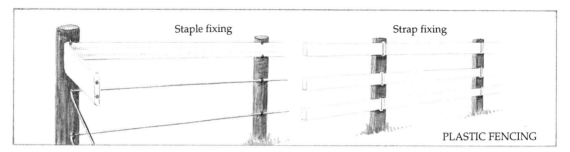

Staple fixing   Strap fixing

PLASTIC FENCING

Plastic fencing consists of tough extruded PVC containing two parallel strands of high tensile 2.50mm fencing wire close to its outer edges. It is available in 3in. (7cm) or 4in. (10cm) widths, and may be white, green, brown or black. The strips are attached to posts by galvanised iron brackets, staples, or strapping.

Plastic fencing looks solid and is very resilient and strong. Easy to erect, it needs little or no maintenance if correctly strained on strong posts. It is more durable than wood as it does not rot, crack or peel, horses will not chew it, and it will absorb strong impact without causing injury. A single strip above a wire fence will make the fence safer and more visible, while three or more lines provide good horse fencing. It will not contain sheep, however. Plastic, or other types of portable fencing, can also be used to make a temporary turn-out paddock, or to protect horses from hazards or trees.

Dangerous fencing

A horse owner is responsible for any damage that a horse does to himself or to others if he gets loose. His field must be safe and secure. Accidents at grass are all too common, but many are avoidable.

Check fences regularly for broken or weak timber, sharp objects like prominent nails, or other hazards. A narrow corner is a potential trap for a bullied horse: it should be rounded off if possible. Strands of loose barbed wire or coils of tangled wire in a field invite disaster. A sagging wire fence, pig/sheep netting, or low strands that a horse could catch his foot in, are all dangerous. Wire must be taut and at least 18ins (46cm) above the ground. If barbed-wire fencing cannot be avoided, make sure there are no loose or broken strands likely to cause serious wounds.

Gates

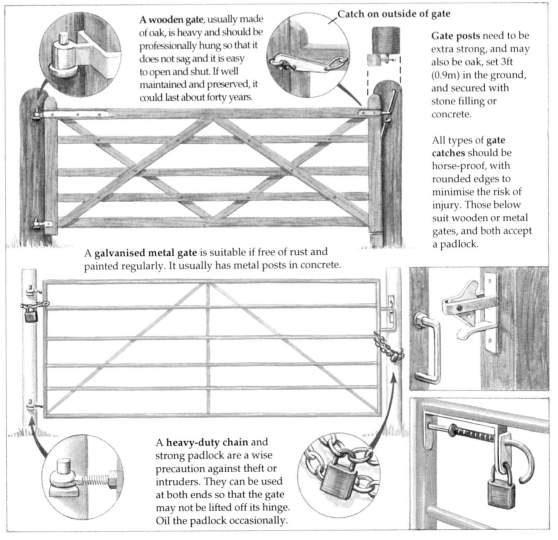

A wooden gate, usually made of oak, is heavy and should be professionally hung so that it does not sag and it is easy to open and shut. If well maintained and preserved, it could last about forty years.

Catch on outside of gate

Gate posts need to be extra strong, and may also be oak, set 3ft (0.9m) in the ground, and secured with stone filling or concrete.

All types of **gate catches** should be horse-proof, with rounded edges to minimise the risk of injury. Those below suit wooden or metal gates, and both accept a padlock.

A **galvanised metal gate** is suitable if free of rust and painted regularly. It usually has metal posts in concrete.

A **heavy-duty chain** and strong padlock are a wise precaution against theft or intruders. They can be used at both ends so that the gate may not be lifted off its hinge. Oil the padlock occasionally.

A field gate must be sturdy, safe, and high enough to be horse-proof, ideally at least 12ft (3.6m) wide, and 4ft (1.2m) high. It should be easy to open with one hand without dragging on the ground, and it must not swing. It is better if a gate opens into a field, to prevent horses or other livestock pushing it open when you unfasten it.

The gate must be designed for horses' safety, with no sharp angles between bars which could trap a foot or leg, causing panic and injury.

Narrow gates are potentially dangerous: if a horse bangs himself on it, he is likely to become gate-shy.

Fastenings must be secure, to withstand heavy pressure, and they must not have prominent sharp edges. Avoid using lightweight metal which is easily bent and damaged, and could therefore cause injury.

Poisonous plants, trees and shrubs

All fields should be kept free from harmful weeds and poisonous vegetation. Weeds such as nettles, docks and thistles rob the soil of its nutritional value and are signs of bad management. Although poisonous weeds such as ragwort and buttercups do not taste good to horses, they might eat them if they are very hungry, or eat the seeds mixed in with the grass. These weeds should therefore be pulled up by the roots and burned. In bad cases they should be killed with chemicals and the field vacated for at least a month. Above all, do not leave cuttings lying about: the wilting or dead plants become not only more palatable, but also much more poisonous, which could lead to sickness and death. Even the healthiest ground can become infected by neighbouring weeds, so check it as often as possible.

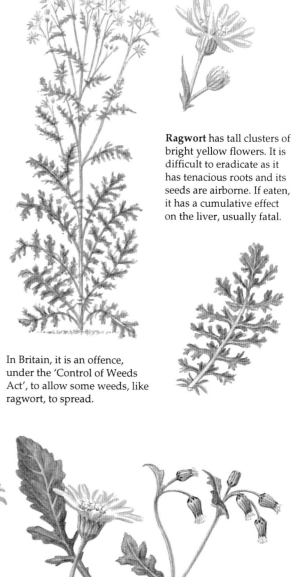

COMMON RAGWORT
Height: 1-4ft (30-120cm)

Ragwort has tall clusters of bright yellow flowers. It is difficult to eradicate as it has tenacious roots and its seeds are airborne. If eaten, it has a cumulative effect on the liver, usually fatal.

In its early stages **ragwort** grows a rosette of leaves. This is the best time to apply a suitable weedkiller to each individual plant.

In Britain, it is an offence, under the 'Control of Weeds Act', to allow some weeds, like ragwort, to spread.

OXFORD RAGWORT
Height: 9-15ins (24-38cm)

HOARY RAGWORT
Height: 1-4ft (30-120cm)

MARSH RAGWORT
Height: 1-4ft (30-120cm)

GROUNDSEL
Height: 3-18ins (8-45cm)

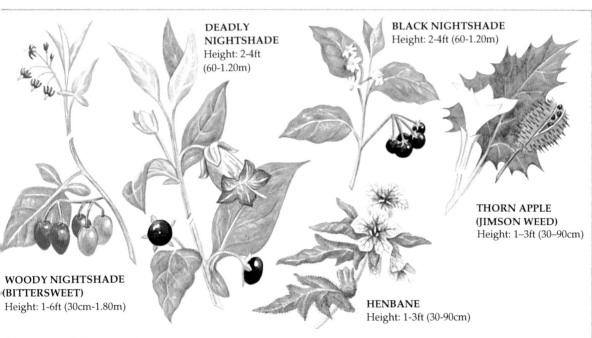

DEADLY NIGHTSHADE
Height: 2-4ft (60-1.20m)

BLACK NIGHTSHADE
Height: 2-4ft (60-1.20m)

THORN APPLE (JIMSON WEED)
Height: 1–3ft (30–90cm)

WOODY NIGHTSHADE (BITTERSWEET)
Height: 1-6ft (30cm-1.80m)

HENBANE
Height: 1-3ft (30-90cm)

All members of the Nightshade family are poisonous to horses, including the greenery of potato and tomato plants.

It is important to recognise all common types of poisonous plant, and to check grazing and hedgerows regularly for new growth. Any toxic plants, such as Deadly Nightshade which has poisonous berries, should be removed completely: if left to die on their own they remain poisonous and could make your horse seriously ill. Also, they may regrow. There is no antidote to Nightshade poisoning. Found in hedges, the plant should be strictly avoided, or it can be sprayed against in early spring.

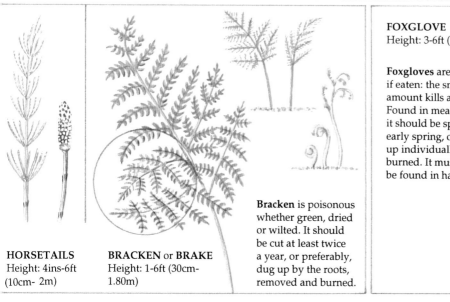

HORSETAILS
Height: 4ins-6ft (10cm- 2m)

BRACKEN or BRAKE
Height: 1-6ft (30cm-1.80m)

Bracken is poisonous whether green, dried or wilted. It should be cut at least twice a year, or preferably, dug up by the roots, removed and burned.

FOXGLOVE
Height: 3-6ft (90- 1.80m)

Foxgloves are lethal if eaten: the smallest amount kills a horse. Found in meadowland, it should be sprayed in early spring, or pulled up individually and burned. It must never be found in hay.

Poisonous plants, trees and shrubs cont.

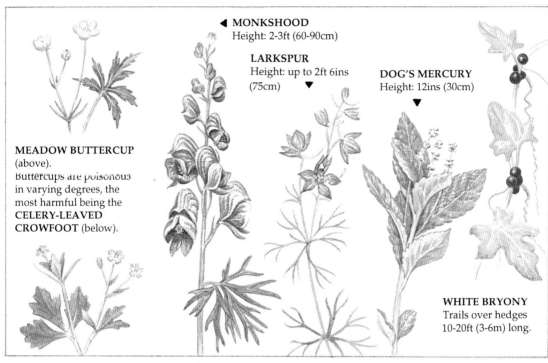

MONKSHOOD
Height: 2-3ft (60-90cm)

LARKSPUR
Height: up to 2ft 6ins
(75cm) ▼

DOG'S MERCURY
Height: 12ins (30cm)
▼

MEADOW BUTTERCUP
(above).
Buttercups are poisonous
in varying degrees, the
most harmful being the
**CELERY-LEAVED
CROWFOOT** (below).

WHITE BRYONY
Trails over hedges
10-20ft (3-6m) long.

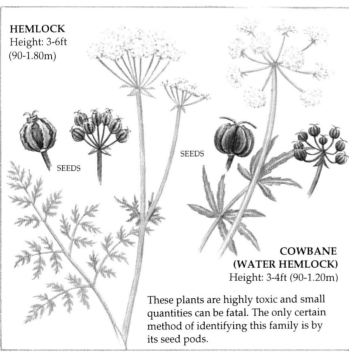

HEMLOCK
Height: 3-6ft
(90-1.80m)

SEEDS

SEEDS

**COWBANE
(WATER HEMLOCK)**
Height: 3-4ft (90-1.20m)

These plants are highly toxic and small
quantities can be fatal. The only certain
method of identifying this family is by
its seed pods.

As with all poisonous plants, the best
time to spray or cut is just after the
new shoot has appeared and before
it comes into bud. If allowed to seed
it will be much more difficult to
eradicate. Small clumps are better
sprayed individually, to minimise
harm to surrounding healthy
vegetation, but large areas of
persistent weeds need applications
of weedkiller by farm machinery.

Other poisonous plants:
FLAX ♦ COLUMBINE ♦ PURPLE
MILK VETCH ♦ LUPINS ♦
YELLOW STAR THISTLE ♦
CROTOLARIA FAMILY ♦
ST JOHN'S WORT ♦ MEADOW
SAFFRON ♦ LOCOWEED ♦
LAUREL ♦ SPURGES ♦ CASTOR
OIL PLANT

Trees:
FALSE ACACIA ♦ RED MAPLE ♦
BLACK WALNUT ♦ WILD
CHERRIES ♦ MAGNOLIA

Acorns, eaten in large quantity, can cause colic with impaction, especially when unripe. The green leaves of oak may also be poisonous in the spring when grass is scarce. Both contain tannic acid. It is advisable to fence off oak trees on grazing land. Crab apples, too, are harmful if too many are eaten.

YEW
Height: up to 70ft (20m)
All parts (dead or living) are poisonous, especially the leaves. No known antidote. Death can be sudden. The commonest form of animal poisoning, as fairly palatable.

LABURNUM
Height: up to 30ft (9m)
Should be safely fenced off from horses. Its seeds are particularly lethal. Beware of twigs, dead or living, which fall or are blown into the field.

PRIVET Height: up to 6ft (2.8m)
Privet, which grows in hedges, is fatally poisonous to horses and there is no known antidote. Its appearance varies from summer to winter, as shown.

OLEANDER and **RHODODENDRON**
Height: 10ft (3m)
These shrubs, and the leaves in particular, contain toxic chemicals that are potentially fatal to horses. They must be fenced off and avoided.

BUCKTHORN
Height: up to 25ft (7.5m)
A shrub or small tree.

15

Field care

To make good use of limited grassland it is necessary to rest, treat and fertilise it periodically.

Horses will not thrive on poor quality land such as wet marshland or a thin new lay; and while lush rich grass may look healthy and appetising to us it may be unpalatable. A large amount of clover or alfalfa in the grass is too rich for most ponies and fat horses. Old established pasture containing a variety of nutritious grasses is best, provided it is well managed.

Droppings should be removed frequently, and weeds eliminated. Coarse, unwanted clumps of grass should be pulled up, cut down, or alternatively, grazed by cattle. Avoid using the field for schooling or jumping if possible as it will reduce productivity. Problems can usually be avoided by dividing up the field and grazing it in rotation. Severely damaged grassland may require ploughing and re-seeding, but such drastic action should be avoidable with careful management. It takes about a year for new turf and grasses to be established for horse grazing, during which time it will need cutting, weed control, and fertilising to encourage the growth of suitable grasses.

Skill is needed to harrow, roll or spray a field, and advice should also be sought if artificial drainage or an appropriate fertiliser is necessary. Harrowing is best done in late February to early April, using a spiked harrow. The ground must be firm, not too wet, to avoid damaging the soil structure. During the summer, chain harrowing aerates the ground and spreads the dung, which helps to kill off larvae. Rolling will level poached or rutted areas, and cutting or 'topping' encourages good growth while keeping weeds in check.

A **harrow** spreads fertiliser and breaks up droppings, killing off worms and parasites. Use it in dry weather. It also allows sun, air and rain to benefit the ground, and fertiliser can be washed in.

A **roller** firms and strengthens pastureland and helps to level poached areas. It can be used about one week after harrowing - and always slowly, as it must not bruise the ground.

Ideal horse pasture contains a variety of grasses and herbs which are palatable, hardy in winter, resistant to hard grazing and cutting, and have varying peak flowering times. Horses will only eat the grasses that they like. They will starve rather than eat sour, rank grass.

A paddock of, say, three acres is at its most nourishing in May and June, and could be grazed by up to ten horses for about two weeks before it may need topping and a three-week break before being grazed again. When growth is slowing down, fields take longer to recover and must not be over-horsed. In winter, supplementary feeding will be necessary.

Very wet, low lying or poorly drained land should not be used during the winter if it can be avoided.

A **cutter bar mower, disc/rotary mower** is used for 'topping' nettles, thistles, and coarse grasses which horses will not eat. Remember, dead weeds are poisonous and must be removed from the field.

Spray as soon as new shoots appear, before they bud.

Dig up persistent weeds with tenacious roots, remove and burn them.

Spraying individual clumps of weeds from a 'back-pack' is the best way to eliminate weeds in small paddocks.

Troublesome weeds commonly found in pasture: **1** PLANTAIN; **2** THISTLE; **3** NETTLE; **4** DOCK. Farm machinery may be needed to spray weeds if they are widespread.

Haymaking

In early summer, grass which is surplus to requirements may be cut for hay. The best 'seed' varieties are purpose grown, while meadow hay is made from permanent pasture. Hay made from grass which has only been grazed by horses is unlikely to be very palatable. Good quality hay has few inferior grasses, and must never contain ragwort or toxic weeds.

Haymaking usually benefits a field. It encourages vigorous growth and undesirable grasses are cut down before they seed. Also, the pasture has a rest from selective grazing, constant treading and unhealthy droppings.

A hay field is usually 'shut off' from mid-April at the latest when it is harrowed, fertilised if necessary, and left to grow. It should be cut before flowering, weather and labour permitting. It is more economical to hire a contractor to make hay on a small acreage, than to buy the machinery. A hay field should be ready for grazing again about four weeks after cutting.

The cut grass is left lying in rows, until the top surface begins to wilt. It is then scattered or turned, dried by sun and wind, then baled when crisp. It is important to remove and stack the bales before it rains!

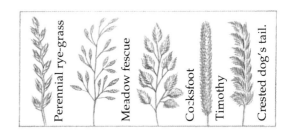

A good mixture of grasses

Perennial rye-grass   Meadow fescue   Cockfoot   Timothy   Crested dog's tail.

Palatable herbage

(a) Dandelion; (b) Ribwort/Ribgrass; (c) Yarrow; (d) Salad burnet; (e) Chicory; (f) White/Dutch clover; (g) Ramsons (wild garlic).These are some of the most beneficial herbs and they should be included in the pasture if possible. They provide variety and horses will seek them out. They are rich in essential minerals such as calcium and they are most nutritious when young and tender.

Field maintenance

If only one field is available for grazing, it will inevitably become horse-sick and worm infested. Ideally, it should be divided up so that one area or strip may be grazed down, then the horses moved to fresh grass while it is topped and treated as necessary. Cattle or sheep will eat the rough clumps that horses leave. The cropped field should then be rested for at least three months.

Where land is in poor condition and horses do not thrive, treatment with appropriate fertiliser is recommended.

To help control worm larvae, and the health and appearance of your field, remove droppings regularly. The water supply must be checked daily, and fencing kept in safe, strong condition. Gateways often become poached in winter, and a load of levelled stone or chalk may help, with water directed away by drainage ditches.

To get the best out of your grazing and to keep worms under control, pick up droppings as often as possible and worm all the horses in the field every six weeks.

Surface water is a sign of inadequate drainage, and ditches may need digging out or cleaning; on poor draining soil, like clay, piped drains under the ground may be necessary.

WARNING: Some wood preservatives are dangerous if inhaled by humans or horses. Check the label before purchase!

Horses may chew wooden gates and fencing when bored, hungry, or deficient in minerals. All timber should be treated with preservative, but make sure it is non-toxic to horses.

Water and troughs

Water is more essential to a horse than food. His body is 70 per cent water, and he needs between 5 and 15 gallons per day, according to the weather, his size and condition, and the moisture in the grass.

Water sources must be kept clean. Watch out for contamination from chemicals, insects, vermin, birds, algae, and leaves (never place a trough beneath deciduous trees).

Whatever trough or container is used, it must have safe, round edges and be strong enough to withstand hard kicks.

If a horse seems to prefer muddy, dirty water to fresh, he may lack minerals.

In winter, ice must be broken at least twice daily. Horses will not break it themselves.

A **stream**, with non-polluted running water, is ideal. It must have a firm, stony or gravel bottom, with easy access at all times of year, otherwise an alternative supply is essential.

Portable water containers are useful for just one or two horses, but make sure they cannot be pushed over. They are easy to move around and to clean, but need constant re-filling.

A **pond** of stagnant (still) water should be fenced off. Such ponds are usually contaminated, boggy and dangerous. Only those which have a natural spring are suitable.

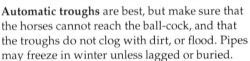

A **water trough** must have safe, easy access for horses, rounded edges, and no dangerous protrusions. It should be raised about 9ins (23cm) above the ground and fixed securely.

Automatic troughs are best, but make sure that the horses cannot reach the ball-cock, and that the troughs do not clog with dirt, or flood. Pipes may freeze in winter unless lagged or buried.

A **badly positioned trough**, too close to the gate, is likely to cause an extremely muddy area. Although it is useful to serve two fields at once, a projecting trough is a hazard.

An **old sink**, or similar container, is adequate provided the water is kept clean, fresh and in plentiful supply. Avoid using old baths or anything sharp-edged, perishable or unstable.

Types of shelter

Horses need some form of shelter from wind, rain or sleet in winter, and from flies and sun in summer. This could be from thick, high hedges, trees, walls, solid fencing, or a shed or building. A solidly constructed and well positioned artificial windbreak is better than no shelter at all.

A hedge with overhanging shade is ideal protection against the elements, and horses often prefer this to a shed. Make sure, though, that it contains nothing poisonous. A belt or clump of evergreen shrubs or trees, such as holly bushes, also provides shelter and a good windbreak at all times of year.

If there is no shelter in your field, and if your horse is not a hardy type, you may have to bring him into a stable when the flies are troublesome, when it is very hot, or in extreme wintry conditions.

Trees can give useful shelter either in a fence line or out in the field, whether one large single tree or a clump or thicket. Low or dead branches should be removed for safety.

A young tree, planted in a field as future shade, will need protection as horses or deer are likely to chew and destroy it. It may be fenced off or surrounded with low voltage live wire.

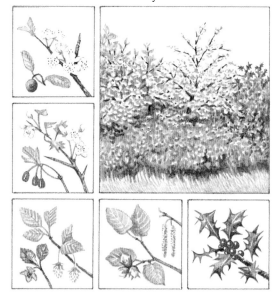

A thick, high hedge provides a good natural windbreak which can also provide shelter and shade. Suitable varieties include blackthorn, hawthorn, beech, hazel, and holly.

Field sheds

A field shelter which is strongly constructed to withstand all weathers and knocks will need minimum maintenance. It should be built on a dry, well-drained part of the field, with its rear wall against the prevailing winds. Its floor should be porous. Deep litter bedding is suitable and it can be put down on to a natural earth base. The doorway must be high and as wide as possible, to encourage horses to use the shed without fear of being trapped in a corner by another horse. On poorly drained land, the floor and entrance area may be concreted, or, alternatively, have stone, rubble or hardened chalk as a base. A shed is useful, too, for feeding hay, out of the wind and rain, but most horses will only use it if it is light and spacious.

A shed, part-walled at the front against wind and rain. The wide doorway provides a safer escape route for a bullied or timid horse. Bedding should be kept clean.

An open-fronted shed of simple and sturdy construction. Note how the roof slopes downwards to the back so that rain water is channelled away behind the shed.

Size: 10ft x 10ft (3m x 3m) is the minimum for one pony; 16ft x 12ft (5m x 3.6m) is suitable for two loose horses.

Checklist

REMEMBER...

VISIT YOUR HORSE AT LEAST ONCE EVERY DAY.

Inspect him closely for any signs of ill-health or injury.

Beware of extremes of temperature, rain, mud, insect bites, bullying.

Boredom and loneliness should be remedied.

A happy horse is easier to look after and a pleasure to own, whereas a discontented, unhealthy horse is not!

As an owner, you are legally responsible if your horse escapes from his field and causes damage to person or property.

FIELD CHECK
- Constant supply of fresh, clean water.
- Healthy grass - plenty to eat.
- Eliminate weeds, worms and poisonous plants.
- Adequate shelter and shade.
- Safety - no holes, litter, sharp objects, loose wires.

FENCING CHECK
- Safe, secure gates. Padlock, where necessary.
- No weak spots.
- No protrusions or hazards, e.g. nails, broken wire or rails.